The Rise of a Dictator: Idi Amin's Journey Through the Ranks of the Ugandan Military

Copyright Page

TITLE: The Rise of a Dictator: Idi Amin's Journey Through the Ranks of the Ugandan Military

1ST Edition

ISBN: 9798223106937

The Rise of a Dictator: Idi Amin's Journey Through the Ranks of the Ugandan Military

By Roberto Miguel Rodriguez

Book Outline

Introduction:

- Briefly introduce the book and its focus on Idi Amin's journey through the ranks of the Ugandan Military.

- Highlight the relevance of understanding Amin's rise to power and its impact on Uganda and African politics.

- Explain that the following subchapters will explore various aspects of Amin's life, regime, and legacy.

Idi Amin's Childhood and Early Life in Uganda:

- Provide a comprehensive overview of Amin's background, including his birth, family, and upbringing in Uganda.

- Discuss any significant events or influences during his formative years that could have shaped his future actions and mindset.

Idi Amin's Rise through the Ranks of the Ugandan Military:

- Trace Amin's military career, from joining the British colonial military to his ascent within the Ugandan military.

- Highlight key milestones, promotions, or achievements that propelled him to power.

- Analyze the tactics and strategies he employed to gain control and consolidate his authority.

Idi Amin's Brutal Regime and Human Rights Abuses:

- Examine the atrocities committed under Amin's regime, including the persecution, torture, and execution of political opponents and civilians.

- Discuss the impact of his policies on human rights, freedom of speech, and democracy in Uganda.

- Explore the psychological and sociopolitical factors that facilitated Amin's brutal reign.

Idi Amin's Relationship with Foreign Powers and International Politics:

- Investigate Amin's alliances, friendships, and rivalries with foreign nations and leaders.

- Analyze how these relationships influenced his decisions, policies, and international standing.

- Discuss the political and diplomatic repercussions of Amin's actions on Uganda's global relations.

Idi Amin's Cultural and Religious Impact on Uganda:

- Explore Amin's promotion of Ugandan nationalism and cultural identity.

- Discuss his efforts to redefine Uganda's cultural and religious landscape, including the expulsion of Asian communities and the promotion of Islam.

- Assess the long-term effects of Amin's cultural and religious policies on the country.

Idi Amin's Economic Policies and their Effects on Uganda's Economy:

- Examine Amin's economic policies, such as nationalization and the expulsion of foreign businesses.

- Assess the impact of these policies on Uganda's economy, including inflation, unemployment, and economic decline.

- Discuss any positive or negative consequences of Amin's economic decisions.

Idi Amin's Military Strategies and Conflicts during his Reign:

- Analyze Amin's military strategies, including his involvement in regional conflicts, such as the Uganda-Tanzania War.

- Discuss his military reforms, recruitment tactics, and relationships with the armed forces.

- Explore the outcomes and consequences of Amin's military actions.

Idi Amin's Exile and Life after Being Overthrown as Dictator:

- Detail Amin's exile in Saudi Arabia and his activities during his time in exile.

- Discuss any attempts to seek justice for his crimes and the international response to his presence in Saudi Arabia.

- Explore his personal life, health, and eventual death.

Idi Amin's Portrayal in Literature, Film, and Popular Culture:

- Examine how Amin has been depicted and portrayed in various forms of media, including books, films, and documentaries.

- Discuss the accuracy and impact of these portrayals on public perception and historical understanding.

Idi Amin's Legacy and Historical Significance in African Politics and Post-Colonial History:

- Evaluate Amin's legacy in Uganda and Africa, including his impact on politics, human rights, and governance.

- Discuss the debates surrounding his historical significance and how he is remembered in post-colonial African history.

- Highlight any lessons or warnings that can be drawn from Amin's rise to power and subsequent reign.

Conclusion:

- Summarize the main points covered in the subchapters.

- Acknowledge the complexity of Amin's life and regime, and the ongoing debates surrounding his legacy.

- Emphasize the importance of studying Amin's journey through the ranks of the Ugandan military to gain insights into African politics and post-colonial history.

Chapter 1: Idi Amin's Childhood and Early Life in Uganda

Family Background and Early Influences

Idi Amin, the notorious dictator of Uganda, was shaped by his family background and early influences, which played a crucial role in molding his character and guiding his path towards power. Understanding these factors is essential to unraveling the complex journey of this dictator, and its implications on African politics and post-colonial history.

Born in 1925 in Koboko, a remote village in northwestern Uganda, Amin was raised in a modest family with a strong tribal background. His father, Andreas Nyabire, was a member of the Kakwa tribe, known for their strong military traditions and warrior heritage. This undoubtedly instilled in Amin a deep sense of pride and the importance of military prowess.

Growing up in a rural setting, Amin experienced firsthand the hardships and inequalities that plagued Uganda during its colonial era. This exposure to poverty and oppression fueled his desire for social justice and empowered him to fight against the injustices he witnessed.

Amin's early life in Uganda also exposed him to the multifaceted religious and cultural landscape of the country. As a Muslim, he embraced Islam and drew inspiration from its teachings, which provided him with a framework for his actions and decisions as a leader. His Muslim identity, combined with his tribal heritage, shaped his worldview and influenced his policies as dictator.

Furthermore, Amin's rise through the ranks of the Ugandan military was propelled by his natural talent as a soldier and his ability to manipulate political dynamics within the military. His military strategies and conflicts during his reign were characterized by a mix of brutality and cunning, which allowed him to consolidate power and maintain control over the country.

The brutal regime of Idi Amin was marked by numerous human rights abuses, including extrajudicial killings, torture, and the persecution of political opponents. These atrocities had a devastating impact on the people of Uganda, leaving scars that are still felt today. Amin's relationship with foreign powers and international politics further contributed to the isolation and economic decline of Uganda during his reign.

After being overthrown as dictator in 1979, Amin lived in exile until his death in 2003. His portrayal in literature, film, and popular culture has perpetuated his image as a ruthless tyrant, ensuring that his legacy lives on in the collective memory of Ugandans and the international community.

In conclusion, understanding Idi Amin's family background and early influences is crucial to comprehending the rise, reign, and fall of this dictator. By analyzing his childhood, cultural and religious impact, military strategies, and human rights abuses, we gain insight into his complex character and the profound impact he had on Uganda and African politics.

Education and Military Training

Idi Amin's journey through the ranks of the Ugandan military was marked by a unique blend of education and military training. This subchapter explores the pivotal role that education played in shaping Amin's rise to power and his subsequent brutal regime.

Idi Amin's childhood and early life in Uganda laid the foundation for his military aspirations. Born to a poor family in Koboko, Amin's education was limited, but he possessed a natural charisma and physical strength that set him apart. It was during his formative years that Amin first encountered the colonial military presence in Uganda, which left a lasting impression on him.

As Amin's military career progressed, his rise through the ranks was fueled by his determination and ability to manipulate those around him. He took advantage of the political instability of post-colonial Uganda, positioning himself as a military leader and gaining support from various factions within the military. Amin's military training, combined with his innate leadership skills, enabled him to seize power in a coup against President Obote in 1971.

Once in power, Amin's regime was characterized by extreme brutality and widespread human rights abuses. His military background allowed him to maintain a tight grip on power, using the military as a tool of repression and control. Amin's disregard for human rights and his brutal tactics tarnished Uganda's international reputation and led to condemnation from the international community.

Amin's relationship with foreign powers and international politics was complex and often unpredictable. He sought alliances with different countries, playing off their rivalries for his own gain. Amin's relationships with foreign powers, such as Libya and Israel, shaped his regime's actions and had far-reaching implications for Uganda and the wider region.

In addition to his military prowess, Amin's cultural and religious impact on Uganda cannot be overlooked. As a Muslim, he sought to promote his own cultural and religious values while suppressing others. This had a significant impact on the social fabric of Uganda and exacerbated existing tensions between different ethnic and religious groups.

Amin's economic policies further compounded the challenges faced by Uganda. His reckless and ill-informed decisions led to the collapse of the economy, with inflation soaring and foreign investments drying up. The consequences of Amin's economic mismanagement were felt long after his regime came to an end.

Throughout his reign, Amin employed military strategies and engaged in conflicts that further destabilized Uganda and the region. His military campaigns, such as the invasion of Tanzania, resulted in thousands of deaths and further isolation from the international community.

Following his overthrow as dictator, Amin lived in exile until his death in 2003. His life after power was marked by attempts to rehabilitate his image and portray himself as a misunderstood leader. However, his brutal legacy and the atrocities committed under his regime overshadowed any attempts at redemption.

Idi Amin's portrayal in literature, film, and popular culture has contributed to his enduring image as a ruthless dictator. Books, movies, and documentaries have sought to capture the horrors of his regime and shed light on the complex personality of this controversial figure.

Amin's legacy and historical significance in African politics and post-colonial history cannot be underestimated. His regime serves as a cautionary tale of the dangers of unchecked military power and the devastating consequences of human rights abuses. Amin's rise to power and subsequent reign continue to shape the political landscape of Uganda and serve as a reminder of the fragility of democracy.

In conclusion, Idi Amin's journey through the ranks of the Ugandan military was intertwined with his education and military training. His rise to power, brutal regime, and subsequent exile left a lasting impact on Uganda and the wider region. Understanding the role of education and military training in Amin's life is crucial to comprehending the complexities of his reign and its lasting historical significance.

Amin's Role in the Colonial Era

Idi Amin, a name that has become synonymous with brutality and tyranny, had a journey that started in the colonial era of Uganda. This subchapter aims to shed light on Amin's role during this crucial period, providing insights into the factors that shaped his later rise to power as a dictator.

Born in 1925 in the West Nile region of Uganda, Amin grew up in a time when Uganda was still under British colonial rule. Like many of his generation, he experienced firsthand the effects of colonialism on his country and its people. This period had a profound impact on his understanding of power dynamics, as he witnessed the exploitation and marginalization of his fellow Ugandans by the British.

Amin's involvement in the colonial era began with his recruitment into the King's African Rifles (KAR), the British colonial army. His rise through the ranks of the military was swift, thanks to his size, strength, and charisma. Amin's military career provided him with a platform to showcase his leadership abilities, and he quickly gained the attention of his superiors.

During this time, Amin's exposure to the inner workings of the colonial administration gave him a unique perspective on governance and control. His interactions with British politicians and diplomats allowed him to witness the mechanisms of power firsthand. Amin learned how to navigate the complex world of politics, acquiring knowledge that would prove invaluable in his subsequent rise to power.

Furthermore, Amin's military training and experiences in the colonial era shaped his approach to leadership. He witnessed the brutal tactics employed by the colonial forces to maintain control, and these experiences influenced his own leadership style. Amin's later regime would be marked by a ruthless and authoritarian approach, mirroring the methods he had observed during his time in the military.

Understanding Amin's role in the colonial era is crucial to grasping the origins of his dictatorship. It was during this period that he acquired the skills, knowledge, and mindset that would propel him to the helm of Uganda's government. By delving into Amin's experiences in the colonial era, politicians and diplomats can gain valuable insights into the complex factors that contributed to his rise, and perhaps, learn from the mistakes of the past to prevent similar tragedies in the future.

In conclusion, Amin's role in the colonial era played a significant part in shaping his later journey through the ranks of the Ugandan military. His exposure to the power dynamics and governance systems during this period influenced his leadership style and provided him with the necessary skills to ascend to the position of dictator. Understanding these formative experiences is vital for politicians and diplomats seeking to comprehend the rise of Idi Amin and the devastating consequences of his reign.

Chapter 2: Idi Amin's Rise through the Ranks of the Ugandan Military

Amin's Entry into the Military

Idi Amin's journey through the ranks of the Ugandan military began with his entry into the armed forces at a young age. Born in Koboko, Uganda, in 1925, Amin experienced a tumultuous childhood marked by poverty and a lack of opportunity. However, his physical strength and charismatic personality soon caught the attention of military recruiters.

At the age of 18, Amin enlisted in the King's African Rifles (KAR), a British-led colonial military force. This marked the beginning of Amin's rise through the ranks, as he quickly distinguished himself as a skilled soldier. His leadership potential and ability to command respect were evident, earning him promotions and increased responsibilities within the KAR.

Amin's time in the military allowed him to develop his military strategies and tactics, which would later play a crucial role in his brutal regime. However, even during his early years, there were signs of his authoritarian tendencies and disregard for human rights. Amin's rise to power was marked by violence and intimidation, and his actions within the military were no exception.

As Amin climbed the military ladder, he established relationships with foreign powers and became involved in international politics. He cultivated alliances with various countries, such as Libya and Saudi Arabia, which provided him with financial and military support. This enabled him to consolidate his power and carry out his brutal regime, characterized by human rights abuses, including torture, extrajudicial killings, and forced disappearances.

Amin's cultural and religious impact on Uganda cannot be overlooked. He imposed his own brand of nationalism, promoting the dominance of the ethnic group he belonged to and marginalizing others. Additionally, he converted to Islam and used religion as a tool to rally support and further divide the population.

Economically, Amin's policies had devastating effects on Uganda's economy. He nationalized industries and expelled foreign businesses, leading to widespread economic decline and a decline in living standards for many Ugandans. The country's infrastructure deteriorated, and corruption became rampant.

During his reign, Amin engaged in military conflicts, such as the invasion of Tanzania and the conflict with Uganda's Asian community. His military strategies were often marked by brutality and a lack of regard for human life. The consequences of these conflicts were felt not only by the Ugandan people but also by neighboring countries.

Amin's dictatorship came to an end when he was overthrown and forced into exile in 1979. His life after being overthrown was marked by a series of failed attempts to regain power and a nomadic existence in various countries. Amin's legacy is a complex one, as he is portrayed in literature, film, and popular culture as a larger-than-life figure, simultaneously feared and ridiculed.

In African politics and post-colonial history, Amin's reign is seen as a cautionary tale of the dangers of unchecked power and the devastating consequences of human rights abuses. His brutal regime left a lasting impact on Uganda, and the scars of his dictatorship are still visible today. Amin's rise through the ranks of the military and his subsequent reign as dictator serve as a stark reminder of the fragility of democracy and the importance of safeguarding human rights.

Rapid Promotions and Leadership Skills

In the subchapter "Rapid Promotions and Leadership Skills" of the book "The Rise of a Dictator: Idi Amin's Journey through the Ranks of the Ugandan Military," we delve into the remarkable ascent of Idi Amin within the Ugandan military and the leadership skills he displayed throughout his rise to power. This chapter aims to provide insights into how Amin's rapid promotions and leadership abilities played a significant role in shaping his brutal regime and his lasting impact on Uganda, African politics, and post-colonial history.

Idi Amin's childhood and early life in Uganda laid the foundation for his military career. Born in rural Uganda, Amin had limited formal education but possessed natural leadership qualities. His charisma and physical prowess caught the attention of British colonial authorities, who recruited him into the King's African Rifles at a young age. Amin quickly rose through the ranks, earning promotions based on his military prowess and ability to command respect from his subordinates.

As Amin climbed the ranks of the Ugandan military, his leadership skills became increasingly apparent. He displayed a unique blend of charm, intimidation, and manipulation, which allowed him to gain the loyalty of his fellow soldiers and secure influential positions. Amin's ability to instill fear and maintain control over his subordinates became a hallmark of his brutal regime.

Furthermore, Amin's leadership skills had a profound impact on his relationship with foreign powers and international politics. His ability to navigate the geopolitical landscape enabled him to gain support from both Western and Eastern bloc countries, playing them against each other to his advantage. Amin's skillful manipulation of international politics allowed him to maintain his grip on power despite his regime's egregious human rights abuses.

This subchapter also explores Amin's cultural and religious impact on Uganda. Amin capitalized on the country's ethnic and religious diversity, using it as a tool to maintain control and divide his opponents. His policies favored certain ethnic and religious groups while marginalizing others, leading to deep-seated divisions within Ugandan society that persist to this day.

Additionally, Amin's economic policies and military strategies during his reign had far-reaching consequences for Uganda's economy and security. His ill-advised economic decisions, such as the expulsion of Asian Ugandans, had devastating effects on the country's economy. Meanwhile, his military strategies and conflicts further destabilized the region, leading to widespread violence and loss of life.

The subchapter also covers Amin's exile and life after being overthrown as dictator. Despite his brutal rule, Amin managed to escape Uganda and lived in various countries until his death. His post-dictatorship life provides insight into the complex psyche of a fallen dictator and the enduring legacy of his actions.

Finally, this subchapter examines how Idi Amin has been portrayed in literature, film, and popular culture. Amin's larger-than-life persona has captivated storytellers, who have sought to understand and depict his rise to power and brutal reign. These portrayals offer different perspectives on Amin's character and actions, contributing to the ongoing discourse surrounding his legacy.

In conclusion, the subchapter "Rapid Promotions and Leadership Skills" sheds light on the remarkable rise of Idi Amin within the Ugandan military, his leadership abilities, and the far-reaching consequences of his actions. It explores Amin's childhood, his military career, his brutal regime, his relationship with foreign powers, his cultural and religious impact, his economic policies, his military strategies and conflicts, his exile and life after being overthrown, his portrayal in popular culture, and his historical significance in African politics and post-colonial history. This chapter aims to provide politicians and diplomats with a comprehensive understanding of Amin's rise to power and the lasting impact he had on Uganda and the wider world.

Amin's Influence on the Military

Idi Amin's journey through the ranks of the Ugandan military was instrumental in shaping his rise to power and his subsequent brutal regime. Amin's childhood and early life in Uganda laid the foundation for his military career, as he developed a reputation for physical strength and bravery. This, combined with his charisma and ability to manipulate those around him, allowed him to climb the military ladder quickly.

As Amin rose through the ranks, he gained control over key military positions and expanded his influence within the armed forces. He fostered a culture of fear and loyalty among his troops, effectively using the military as a tool to consolidate his power. His ruthless tactics and human rights abuses became a hallmark of his regime, as he silenced dissent and carried out mass killings, torture, and other atrocities.

Despite his brutal domestic policies, Amin maintained relationships with foreign powers and played a role in international politics. He strategically aligned Uganda with countries such as Libya and the Soviet Union, while also cultivating relationships with Western nations. His ability to navigate international alliances allowed him to secure economic aid and military support for his regime.

Amin's cultural and religious impact on Uganda cannot be understated. He implemented policies that favored his own ethnic group, the Kakwa, leading to widespread discrimination and persecution of other tribes. Additionally, Amin's conversion to Islam and his close ties with the Arab world further polarized the country along religious lines.

Economically, Amin's policies had disastrous effects on Uganda's economy. His nationalization of industries and expulsion of Asian business owners led to a collapse in productivity and foreign investment.

The country faced severe economic decline, with skyrocketing inflation and widespread poverty.

Amin's military strategies and conflicts during his reign also had a significant impact. He invaded Tanzania in 1978, leading to a costly and disastrous war that further weakened his regime. His military campaigns were marked by incompetence, as he prioritized personal glory over strategic planning.

After being overthrown as dictator, Amin lived in exile but continued to maintain a presence in international media. His portrayal in literature, film, and popular culture often depicted him as a cartoonish villain, further cementing his infamy.

Amin's legacy and historical significance in African politics and post-colonial history cannot be denied. His brutal regime and human rights abuses serve as a cautionary tale of unchecked power and the dangers of authoritarianism. Amin's reign highlighted the need for international intervention in cases of severe human rights violations and set a precedent for international criminal tribunals.

In conclusion, Amin's influence on the military shaped his rise to power and his subsequent brutal regime. His childhood and early life laid the foundation for his military career, and his charisma and manipulation skills allowed him to quickly climb the ranks. Amin's brutal regime and human rights abuses, his relationships with foreign powers, his cultural and religious impact, his disastrous economic policies, his military strategies and conflicts, his life after being overthrown, his portrayal in media, and his lasting legacy all contribute to a comprehensive understanding of his impact on African politics and post-colonial history.

Chapter 3: Idi Amin's Brutal Regime and Human Rights Abuses

Amin's Seizure of Power and Consolidation of Control

Idi Amin's seizure of power in Uganda marked a turning point in the nation's history and had far-reaching implications for African politics and post-colonial history. This subchapter explores the events that led to Amin's rise to power and his subsequent consolidation of control over the country.

Born in Koboko, a small village in northwest Uganda, Amin's childhood and early life were marked by poverty and struggle. However, his talent for boxing caught the attention of British colonial officials, who recruited him into the King's African Rifles (KAR), the colonial army. Amin quickly rose through the ranks, benefiting from British training and support.

As Amin climbed the military ladder, his ambition and ruthlessness became evident. Exploiting political turmoil and divisions within the Ugandan government, Amin orchestrated a coup in 1971 that toppled President Obote from power. Amin's brutal regime and human rights abuses during his rule are notorious, with estimates suggesting that up to half a million people were killed under his regime. This subchapter delves into the atrocities committed by Amin's regime, shedding light on the horrifying realities faced by Ugandans during this dark period.

Amin's relationship with foreign powers and international politics also played a significant role in his consolidation of control. He sought to portray himself as a pan-African leader, often using anti-colonial rhetoric to gain support from other African nations. However, his erratic behavior, expulsion of Asian minorities, and growing isolation from the international community strained Uganda's relations with foreign powers.

The chapter further explores Amin's cultural and religious impact on Uganda. Amin's regime promoted a militaristic and nationalistic ideology that sought to redefine Ugandan identity and erase colonial influences. This subchapter delves into his efforts to reshape the nation's cultural and religious landscape, often through force and coercion.

Additionally, Amin's economic policies and their effects on Uganda's economy are examined. Amin's mismanagement and corruption led to a severe economic decline, with inflation skyrocketing and foreign investment dwindling. This subchapter provides an analysis of his economic strategies and their devastating consequences for the country.

Furthermore, Amin's military strategies and conflicts during his reign are explored. Amin engaged in several military campaigns, including the invasion of Tanzania, which proved disastrous for Uganda. The subchapter delves into Amin's military tactics, his relationship with the military, and the conflicts that defined his rule.

Finally, the subchapter concludes by examining Amin's exile and life after being overthrown as dictator. It also delves into how Amin has been portrayed in literature, film, and popular culture, shedding light on the diverse interpretations and representations of his character and actions.

In summary, Amin's seizure of power and consolidation of control had a profound impact on Uganda and African politics. This subchapter provides a comprehensive analysis of the events and factors that shaped Amin's rise to power, his brutal regime, and his enduring legacy. It serves as a valuable resource for politicians, diplomats, and anyone interested in understanding the complexities of African politics and post-colonial history.

State-Sponsored Violence and Political Repression

Throughout the reign of Idi Amin, Uganda witnessed an unprecedented wave of state-sponsored violence and political repression. This subchapter delves into the dark and brutal aspects of Amin's regime, shedding light on the human rights abuses that plagued the nation during his rule. Addressed to politicians and diplomats, this chapter aims to provide a comprehensive understanding of the impact of Amin's regime on Uganda and its people.

Idi Amin's rise through the ranks of the Ugandan military laid the foundation for his brutal regime. Born in rural Uganda, Amin's childhood and early life shaped his worldview and aspirations. His military prowess catapulted him into power, allowing him to establish an iron-fisted grip on the nation's politics. The subchapter examines the strategies Amin employed to consolidate his power and the detrimental consequences these had on Uganda's political landscape.

Under Amin's rule, human rights abuses reached alarming proportions. From political dissidents to ethnic minorities, no section of society was spared from the regime's barbarity. The subchapter explores the methods employed by Amin's government to silence opposition, including torture, extrajudicial killings, and mass displacement. It also highlights the impact of these abuses on the social fabric of Uganda, leaving scars that persist to this day.

Amin's relationship with foreign powers and international politics played a crucial role in sustaining his regime. The subchapter delves into the alliances Amin forged with various nations and the consequences of these partnerships. It also analyzes the international community's response to Amin's human rights abuses, including the diplomatic and economic sanctions imposed on Uganda.

Beyond politics, Amin's cultural and religious impact on Uganda cannot be ignored. His policies favored his own ethnic group, exacerbating ethnic tensions within the country. The chapter delves into Amin's manipulation of religion and culture to further his political agenda, exploring the long-lasting repercussions on Ugandan society.

Furthermore, this subchapter investigates the economic policies implemented by Amin and their devastating effects on Uganda's economy. Mismanagement, corruption, and nationalization policies led to economic decline and widespread poverty, impacting the lives of ordinary Ugandans.

Lastly, the subchapter explores Amin's military strategies and conflicts during his reign, shedding light on his aggressive stance towards neighboring countries and the consequences of his military adventurism.

By examining Amin's exile and life after being overthrown as dictator, this subchapter also offers insights into the complexities of post-authoritarian politics. It analyzes the portrayal of Amin in literature, film, and popular culture and reflects on the dictator's legacy and historical significance in African politics and post-colonial history.

In conclusion, this subchapter serves as a comprehensive analysis of the state-sponsored violence and political repression witnessed in Uganda during Idi Amin's reign. It provides a valuable resource for politicians, diplomats, and scholars seeking to understand the intricate dynamics of Amin's regime and its enduring impact on Uganda and beyond.

Amin's Infamous Actions and International Condemnation

Idi Amin's reign as the dictator of Uganda marked one of the darkest chapters in African history. His brutal regime and human rights abuses shocked the world and led to widespread international condemnation. This subchapter delves into Amin's infamous actions and the reactions from foreign powers, shedding light on the impact of his rule on the global stage.

Throughout his rule, Amin demonstrated a complete disregard for human life and dignity. His regime was characterized by widespread torture, extrajudicial killings, and the persecution of political opponents. Amin's reign was marked by a reign of terror, leaving thousands dead and countless others scarred for life. These actions drew the attention of politicians and diplomats worldwide, who were appalled by the atrocities committed under his leadership.

The international community, including the United Nations and various human rights organizations, vehemently condemned Amin's actions. Numerous resolutions and statements were issued, calling for an end to the human rights abuses and demanding justice for the victims. Many countries imposed economic sanctions on Uganda, isolating Amin and his regime from the rest of the world.

Amin's relationship with foreign powers further complicated matters. Despite his brutal regime, he managed to maintain alliances with certain countries, primarily through his strategic manipulation of international politics. Amin skillfully played off rivalries between major powers, exploiting Cold War tensions to his advantage. This allowed him to receive support and military aid from various countries, further enabling his oppressive rule.

The impact of Amin's actions extended beyond politics and human rights. His rule had profound cultural and religious implications for Uganda. Amin implemented policies that favored his own ethnic group and suppressed others, leading to ethnic tensions and divisions within the country. Additionally, he attempted to impose his own version of Islam on the population, further alienating different religious communities and exacerbating social unrest.

Economically, Amin's policies were disastrous for Uganda. His nationalization efforts and reckless fiscal management led to the collapse of the economy, resulting in skyrocketing inflation, widespread poverty, and a decline in foreign investment. The consequences of his economic mismanagement continue to be felt in Uganda to this day.

Amin's military strategies and conflicts during his reign also warrant attention. His aggressive foreign policies, including the invasion of neighboring Tanzania, further strained relations with the international community. Amin's military adventures not only resulted in significant loss of life but also further isolated him diplomatically.

After being overthrown as dictator, Amin lived in exile. His life during this period was marked by obscurity, as he struggled to regain the power and influence he once held. Amin's portrayal in literature, film, and popular culture has been a subject of interest, with various works attempting to capture the complexities of his character and the horrors of his regime.

Amin's legacy and historical significance in African politics and post-colonial history cannot be understated. His reign serves as a stark reminder of the dangers of unchecked power and the importance of upholding human rights. Amin's actions and the international condemnation they sparked continue to shape discussions on accountability, transitional justice, and the role of the international community in preventing atrocities.

In conclusion, Amin's infamous actions and the international condemnation they elicited provide a chilling account of one of the most brutal dictators in African history. This subchapter highlights the significance of his reign on various aspects, from human rights abuses and political relations to cultural, religious, and economic consequences. The lessons learned from Amin's rule continue to inform our understanding of the complexities of power and the importance of safeguarding human rights in the face of tyranny.

Chapter 4: Idi Amin's Relationship with Foreign Powers and International Politics

Amin's Geopolitical Maneuvering and Alliances

Throughout his reign as dictator of Uganda, Idi Amin strategically navigated the complex web of geopolitics and formed alliances that both secured his power and allowed him to play a significant role in international politics. Amin's understanding of global affairs and his ability to manipulate various foreign powers contributed to his continued grip on power despite his brutal regime and human rights abuses.

One of Amin's key geopolitical maneuvers was his alignment with the Arab world. By positioning himself as a champion of Arab causes and an opponent of Israel, Amin sought to gain support and financial aid from Arab nations. This alliance not only provided him with much-needed economic resources but also allowed him to project himself as a prominent figure on the international stage.

Amin's relationship with Libya's Muammar Gaddafi was particularly noteworthy. The two leaders shared a common disdain for Western imperialism and formed a close bond. Gaddafi provided Amin with military and financial assistance, while Amin, in turn, supported Gaddafi's pan-Africanist agenda. This alliance not only bolstered Amin's military capabilities but also allowed him to exert influence beyond Uganda's borders.

Additionally, Amin cultivated ties with other African nations, particularly those seeking independence or struggling against colonial rule. By positioning himself as a leader against Western imperialism, Amin gained support from African nations and established himself as a key player in the Pan-African movement. This enabled him to meddle in the affairs of neighboring countries, further expanding his influence and power.

However, Amin's alliances were not limited to African and Arab nations. He also sought support from Western powers, particularly during the Cold War era. Amin skillfully played off the ideological rivalries between the United States and the Soviet Union, receiving aid from both superpowers at different points in time. This allowed him to maintain a delicate balance and extract maximum benefits from his relationships with these global powers.

Amin's geopolitical maneuvering had far-reaching consequences for Uganda and the African continent as a whole. His brutal regime and human rights abuses tarnished the image of African leaders and undermined efforts to establish stable governments. Moreover, his economic policies, characterized by corruption and mismanagement, devastated Uganda's economy, leaving the country in a state of near collapse.

Despite his eventual exile and the end of his dictatorial rule, Amin's legacy and historical significance in African politics and post-colonial history cannot be ignored. His ability to navigate the complexities of international politics and his skillful manipulation of foreign powers continue to serve as a cautionary tale for politicians and diplomats around the world. Amin's reign serves as a stark reminder of the dangers of unchecked power and the impact of geopolitics on nations and their people.

Amin's Impact on Regional Politics and African Unity

Idi Amin's reign as the dictator of Uganda from 1971 to 1979 had profound implications not only for the people of Uganda but also for regional politics and African unity. Amin's actions and policies during his time in power shaped the political landscape of East Africa and left a lasting impact on the continent as a whole.

One of the key aspects of Amin's rule was his aggressive foreign policy, which had significant consequences for regional politics. Amin sought to establish Uganda as a major player in East Africa and actively pursued alliances with other African nations. He supported various liberation movements, providing them with arms, training, and logistical support. This interventionist approach both enhanced Uganda's influence in the region and fueled conflicts, particularly in neighboring countries such as Tanzania and Kenya.

Amin's regime was notorious for its brutal human rights abuses, which further strained regional relationships and African unity. The mass killings, torture, and persecution carried out by his security forces resulted in a wave of refugees fleeing Uganda and seeking asylum in neighboring countries. This created tensions between Uganda and its neighbors and strained diplomatic relations.

Furthermore, Amin's relationship with foreign powers and his involvement in international politics had far-reaching consequences. He often played one power against another, exploiting Cold War rivalries to his advantage. Amin cultivated relationships with both the United States and the Soviet Union, receiving military aid from both sides. However, his erratic behavior and unpredictable policies made him a liability for foreign powers, who eventually distanced themselves from his regime.

Amin's cultural and religious impact on Uganda cannot be overlooked. He promoted Islam as the state religion and favored Muslims in his government, which created divisions along religious lines. Additionally, Amin's policies targeted certain ethnic groups, leading to further social and cultural fractures within Ugandan society.

From an economic perspective, Amin's policies were disastrous for Uganda. His nationalization of industries and expulsion of Asian minorities severely damaged the economy, leading to rampant inflation, food shortages, and economic decline.

In terms of military strategies and conflicts, Amin's regime was marked by aggression and expansionism. He invaded neighboring Tanzania in 1978, leading to a brief but bloody war that eventually resulted in his downfall. Amin's military adventures not only destabilized the region but also highlighted his disregard for international norms and regional stability.

After being overthrown as dictator, Amin lived in exile until his death in 2003. His portrayal in literature, film, and popular culture has often emphasized his brutality and eccentricity, further cementing his reputation as one of Africa's most infamous dictators.

Idi Amin's legacy and historical significance in African politics and post-colonial history cannot be underestimated. His rule highlighted the challenges of post-colonial governance and the dangers of unchecked power. Amin's actions had a lasting impact on regional politics, African unity, and the perception of African leaders on the international stage. It serves as a reminder of the importance of good governance, human rights, and the pursuit of social and economic development for the stability and progress of African nations.

Amin's Expulsion of Certain Ethnic and Foreign Groups

Subchapter: Amin's Expulsion of Certain Ethnic and Foreign Groups

In the tumultuous era of Idi Amin's reign as dictator in Uganda, one of the darkest chapters was his expulsion of certain ethnic and foreign groups. This subchapter explores the horrifying impact of Amin's policies on these marginalized communities, shedding light on the historical significance of this period in African politics and post-colonial history.

Amin's brutal regime targeted several ethnic groups, most notably the Acholi, Lango, and the Asian community. These communities bore the brunt of Amin's discriminatory policies, which resulted in mass displacement, violence, and loss of life. Amin's actions were marked by ethnic cleansing, resulting in the expulsion of thousands of Ugandans from their homes.

The expulsion of the Asian community, who had played a significant role in Uganda's economy, had severe economic repercussions. Amin's misguided economic policies and demonization of foreigners led to the collapse of businesses and a significant decline in Uganda's economy. This not only affected the livelihoods of the expelled Asians but also had long-lasting consequences for the country as a whole.

Amin's expulsion policies also strained Uganda's relationship with foreign powers and triggered international condemnation. Diplomats and politicians from around the world witnessed the atrocities committed under Amin's regime, leading to strained diplomatic relations and economic isolation for Uganda.

Furthermore, Amin's expulsion policies had a profound cultural and religious impact on Uganda. The diverse tapestry of Ugandan society was torn apart, and the country's cultural and religious fabric was irreparably damaged. Communities that had coexisted peacefully for generations were forcibly separated, leaving scars that still persist today.

The subchapter also delves into Amin's military strategies and conflicts during his reign. Amin's military background played a pivotal role in his rise to power and his ability to maintain control over Uganda. By exploring his military strategies, readers gain insight into the tactics employed by Amin to suppress dissent and perpetuate his brutal regime.

Finally, this subchapter examines the legacy of Amin's expulsion policies and his overall impact on Ugandan society. It explores how his actions continue to shape the political landscape of Uganda and have left an indelible mark on the country's history. Furthermore, it delves into the portrayal of Amin in literature, film, and popular culture, shedding light on the various narratives that have emerged surrounding this controversial figure.

In conclusion, Amin's expulsion of certain ethnic and foreign groups during his reign as dictator left an indelible mark on Uganda's history. This subchapter provides a comprehensive understanding of the impact of these policies, highlighting the historical significance of Amin's regime and its lasting consequences on Ugandan society. It serves as a crucial resource for politicians, diplomats, and anyone seeking a deeper understanding of Idi Amin's journey through the ranks of the Ugandan military and his subsequent reign of terror.

Chapter 5: Idi Amin's Cultural and Religious Impact on Uganda

Amin's Promotion of Ugandan Cultural Nationalism

Idi Amin, the notorious dictator of Uganda, rose to power in the early 1970s and imposed his brutal regime on the country for nearly a decade. Throughout his reign, Amin made significant efforts to promote Ugandan cultural nationalism, a strategy aimed at consolidating his power and fostering a sense of national identity among the people.

Amin, born in Koboko, West Nile Province, Uganda, grew up in a diverse cultural environment that influenced his perspective on national identity. He was of the Kakwa ethnic group, but his exposure to various tribal traditions and beliefs shaped his understanding of Ugandan culture as a whole. This upbringing had a profound impact on Amin's later policies and actions as he sought to unite the country under a common cultural identity.

As Amin rose through the ranks of the Ugandan military, he used his position to promote and enforce cultural nationalism. He implemented policies that emphasized the importance of Ugandan traditions, customs, and languages, often elevating his own Kakwa culture to a prominent position. Amin encouraged the celebration of cultural festivals, the preservation of traditional practices, and the use of local languages in education and administration.

However, Amin's promotion of cultural nationalism was not solely driven by a desire to unite the country. It was also a tool to consolidate his power and suppress dissent. Amin's regime used cultural nationalism as a means to marginalize ethnic groups that were perceived as threats to his authority. This led to widespread human rights abuses, with targeted violence and discrimination against minority communities.

Amin's relationship with foreign powers and international politics also influenced his promotion of cultural nationalism. He often used anti-colonial rhetoric and portrayed himself as a defender of African identity against Western imperialism. This resonated with many African politicians and diplomats, who saw Amin as a symbol of resistance against colonial legacies.

Despite his efforts, Amin's brutal regime and human rights abuses overshadowed his promotion of cultural nationalism. His economic policies, characterized by corruption and mismanagement, led to the collapse of Uganda's economy, causing widespread suffering among the population.

Amin's exile and life after being overthrown as a dictator marked the end of his reign, but his legacy and historical significance in African politics and post-colonial history remain. His brutal regime and promotion of cultural nationalism continue to be subjects of study and debate, shedding light on the complexities of power, identity, and nationalism in African nations.

In literature, film, and popular culture, Amin's portrayal has been both a source of fascination and controversy. Numerous books, documentaries, and movies have explored his life and regime, often highlighting the atrocities committed under his rule.

Overall, Amin's promotion of Ugandan cultural nationalism was a complex and multi-faceted strategy that aimed to unite the country and consolidate his power. However, the brutal methods and human rights abuses associated with his regime have overshadowed his efforts, leaving a legacy that continues to shape the understanding of African politics and post-colonial history.

Amin's Religious Policies and Influence on Islam

During his brutal regime, Idi Amin implemented various religious policies that had a profound impact on Islam in Uganda. Amin, who was a Muslim himself, sought to consolidate his power and maintain control over the country by using religion as a tool of manipulation and oppression.

One of Amin's first steps was to promote Islam as the dominant religion in Uganda. He sought to expand the influence of Islam by building mosques, promoting Islamic education, and encouraging conversions to Islam. This led to a significant increase in the number of Muslims in Uganda, as well as the rise of Islamic institutions and organizations.

Amin also used religion to justify his violent and oppressive actions. He claimed to be a defender of Islam and used religious rhetoric to gain support and loyalty from the Muslim community. Amin often portrayed himself as a devout Muslim, attending Friday prayers and publicly practicing Islamic rituals. However, his actions contradicted the teachings of Islam, as he engaged in widespread human rights abuses and violence against his own people.

Furthermore, Amin's policies and actions led to a radicalization of Islam in Uganda. Under his regime, extremist ideologies started to take root, leading to the emergence of radical Islamic groups. These groups, inspired by Amin's oppressive tactics, sought to further their own agendas through violence and terrorism.

Internationally, Amin's religious policies had an impact on Uganda's relationship with foreign powers. Some countries, particularly those with Muslim-majority populations, supported Amin's regime due to his promotion of Islam. However, other nations condemned his actions and human rights abuses, leading to strained diplomatic relations.

Amin's religious policies also had economic consequences. His focus on Islam and promotion of Islamic institutions resulted in neglect of other important sectors of the economy. This led to economic decline, as resources were diverted to support religious endeavors rather than infrastructure development or social welfare programs.

Today, Amin's religious policies continue to have a lasting impact on Uganda. The radicalization of Islam that occurred during his regime has had long-term consequences, with extremist groups still present in the country. Additionally, the legacy of Amin's oppressive tactics and manipulation of religion continues to shape Uganda's political and social landscape.

In conclusion, Amin's religious policies had a significant influence on Islam in Uganda. His promotion of Islam, coupled with his use of religion to justify violence and repression, led to a radicalization of the faith and the emergence of extremist groups. Amin's policies also had economic consequences and strained Uganda's international relations. Today, his religious legacy continues to shape Uganda's political and social landscape, making it an important aspect of his overall historical significance in African politics and post-colonial history.

Amin's Suppression of Cultural and Religious Dissent

Title: Amin's Suppression of Cultural and Religious Dissent: A Dark Stain on Uganda's History

Introduction:

In the tumultuous history of Uganda, one dictatorial regime stands out for its ruthlessness and the immense suffering it inflicted upon its people. Idi Amin's reign as dictator represents a chapter of horror and oppression that scarred the nation's cultural and religious fabric. This subchapter delves into the systematic suppression of dissenting voices under Amin's brutal regime, shedding light on the devastating consequences it had on Uganda's identity and social harmony.

Cultural Repression:

Idi Amin's regime was marked by the systematic repression of cultural diversity within Uganda. Amin, driven by his own narrow worldview, sought to impose a homogenous national identity. He targeted ethnic groups, banning their traditional practices, and punishing those who dared to celebrate their cultural heritage. This suppression resulted in the loss of cultural richness and diversity that had been the essence of Uganda for centuries.

Religious Persecution:

Under Amin's regime, religious freedom was brutally curtailed. Amin targeted religious institutions and leaders, particularly those who criticized or challenged his authority. Churches, mosques, and temples became targets of violence, with countless innocent lives lost. This assault on religious freedom shattered the spiritual fabric of Uganda, leading to widespread fear and mistrust among its diverse religious communities.

Impact on Society:

The suppression of cultural and religious dissent had a profound impact on Ugandan society. Amin's regime sowed the seeds of division and distrust, pitting ethnic groups and religious communities against one another. The social harmony that had once characterized Uganda was shattered, leaving wounds that would take years to heal. Communities were torn apart, friendships severed, and a sense of unity was replaced by fear and suspicion.

International Response:

The international community, including politicians and diplomats, watched in horror as Amin's atrocities unfolded. Despite widespread condemnation, foreign powers struggled to effectively address the situation due to their own geopolitical interests. This chapter explores

Amin's complex relationship with foreign powers and sheds light on the complicity that allowed his reign of terror to persist.

Legacy and Historical Significance:

Idi Amin's legacy continues to cast a long shadow over Uganda's history and African politics. His brutal regime left an indelible mark on the nation's cultural and religious landscape, a scar that is still healing today. This subchapter examines Amin's lasting impact on Uganda's post-colonial history, the ongoing struggles for reconciliation, and the lessons learned from this dark chapter in African politics.

Conclusion:

The suppression of cultural and religious dissent under Idi Amin's regime remains a painful reminder of the horrors inflicted upon Uganda. This subchapter serves as a stark reminder of the importance of safeguarding cultural and religious diversity, and the need to protect and promote human rights in the face of tyranny. By understanding and learning from this dark period in history, politicians and diplomats can strive to ensure that such atrocities are never repeated.

Chapter 6: Idi Amin's Economic Policies and their Effects on Uganda's Economy

Amin's Nationalization and Economic Mismanagement

In this subchapter, we delve into one of the most significant aspects of Idi Amin's rule - his economic policies and their detrimental effects on Uganda's economy. Amin's nationalization and economic mismanagement led to severe consequences that are still felt in the country today.

Upon assuming power, Amin implemented a policy of nationalization, seizing control of key industries such as banking, manufacturing, and agriculture. This move was intended to promote economic independence and reduce foreign influence. However, instead of bringing prosperity, Amin's nationalization efforts resulted in economic collapse and widespread poverty.

Under his regime, mismanagement and corruption became rampant. Inexperienced individuals were appointed to key positions solely based on loyalty to the regime, leading to a lack of expertise and efficiency in running these industries. As a result, productivity plummeted, and businesses struggled to stay afloat.

Furthermore, Amin's expulsion of the Asian community, who played a crucial role in Uganda's economy, worsened the economic crisis. These individuals, who were predominantly involved in trade and business, were forced to leave the country, taking their skills and capital with them. This exodus left a void that was not easily filled, and the economy suffered as a result.

Amin's economic policies also led to hyperinflation, with the value of the Ugandan shilling plummeting. Basic commodities became scarce, and the cost of living skyrocketed, pushing many Ugandans further into poverty.

Despite the economic downturn, Amin continued to spend recklessly, diverting funds meant for development into personal projects and military spending. The military, which was already bloated and ill-equipped, became a significant drain on the economy.

As a result of Amin's economic mismanagement, Uganda's GDP plummeted, and the country became heavily dependent on foreign aid. It took years for the economy to recover, and even today, Uganda is still grappling with the aftermath of Amin's disastrous economic policies.

In conclusion, Amin's nationalization and economic mismanagement had devastating consequences for Uganda's economy. His policies resulted in economic collapse, hyperinflation, and widespread poverty. The expulsion of the Asian community further crippled the economy, while Amin's reckless spending exacerbated the crisis. It is crucial for politicians and diplomats to study this aspect of Amin's reign to understand the long-lasting effects of economic mismanagement and the importance of sound economic policies in nation-building.

Amin's Impact on Agriculture and Industrial Sectors

Idi Amin's regime in Uganda left a lasting impact on various sectors of the country's economy, including agriculture and industry. During his time in power, Amin implemented policies that significantly affected the agricultural and industrial sectors, leading to economic decline and hardship for the Ugandan people.

One of Amin's major economic policies was the forced expulsion of Asian Ugandans in 1972. This decision had a devastating effect on the agricultural sector, as many of the expelled Asians were skilled farmers who had played a crucial role in Uganda's agricultural development.

Their departure resulted in a significant decrease in agricultural production, leading to food shortages and soaring prices.

Furthermore, Amin's policies of nationalization and state control negatively impacted the industrial sector. He seized control of numerous industries, including large foreign-owned companies, and placed them under state control. The lack of expertise and mismanagement led to a decline in productivity and quality, causing many industries to collapse. The nationalization also discouraged foreign investment and hindered technological advancements, further crippling the industrial sector.

Moreover, Amin's brutal regime and human rights abuses had a profound impact on both agriculture and industry. His reign was marked by violence, corruption, and fear, which created an atmosphere of instability and uncertainty. This climate of fear deterred foreign investors and skilled professionals from engaging in the agricultural and industrial sectors, further exacerbating the economic decline.

Amin's economic policies and mismanagement also led to hyperinflation, with prices skyrocketing and the value of the Ugandan currency plummeting. This inflationary environment made it increasingly difficult for farmers and industrialists to operate, as the cost of inputs and materials became exorbitant. As a result, both sectors faced severe challenges, hindering their growth and development.

Despite these negative consequences, it is important to note that Amin's impact on agriculture and industry extended beyond his time in power. His policies and actions left a lasting legacy, influencing subsequent governments' approach to economic development. The subsequent administrations had to undertake significant efforts to revive these sectors and restore confidence among investors.

In conclusion, Idi Amin's regime had a detrimental impact on Uganda's agriculture and industrial sectors. His policies, including the expulsion of Asian Ugandans and state control of industries, led to a decline in production, a collapse of industries, and hyperinflation. The consequences of Amin's actions were felt long after his rule, requiring subsequent governments to work towards rebuilding these sectors and restoring economic stability.

Amin's Legacy on Uganda's Economic Development

Idi Amin, the notorious dictator who ruled Uganda from 1971 to 1979, left a lasting legacy on the country's economic development. During his brutal regime, Amin implemented a series of economic policies that had far-reaching consequences for Uganda's economy, both during his reign and in the years that followed.

One of Amin's first economic actions was the expulsion of Asians from Uganda, which had a significant impact on the country's economy. The Asian community, predominantly engaged in trade and commerce, played a vital role in Uganda's economy. Their forced exodus resulted in the collapse of many businesses and a decline in economic productivity. The void left by the Asians was never adequately filled, and it took years for Uganda's economy to recover from this blow.

Amin's economic policies were characterized by mismanagement, corruption, and favoritism. He nationalized key industries, including banking, agriculture, and manufacturing, under the pretext of promoting economic independence. However, the state-run enterprises were plagued by inefficiency and lack of expertise, resulting in a decline in productivity and output. Furthermore, Amin's regime was notorious for its rampant corruption, with government officials embezzling public funds and engaging in illicit activities for personal gain.

The economic consequences of Amin's misrule were severe. Inflation soared, reaching unprecedented levels, and the value of the Ugandan currency plummeted. The country faced a severe shortage of foreign exchange, making it difficult to import essential goods and services. The agricultural sector, which was once the backbone of Uganda's economy, suffered greatly due to neglect and mismanagement. Food scarcity became a pressing issue, exacerbating the already dire economic situation.

Amin's economic policies also had a detrimental effect on foreign investment and international trade. His erratic behavior and human rights abuses deterred foreign investors, who were wary of the unstable political climate. As a result, Uganda's economy stagnated, and the country became isolated from the international community.

Despite the devastating impact of Amin's economic policies, it is essential to acknowledge the efforts made by subsequent Ugandan governments to rebuild and revive the economy. Since Amin's downfall, Uganda has made significant strides in economic development, focusing on areas such as agriculture, tourism, and infrastructure. However, the scars left by Amin's misrule are still visible, and the country continues to grapple with the long-lasting effects of his economic policies.

Amin's legacy on Uganda's economic development serves as a cautionary tale for politicians and diplomats. It highlights the importance of sound economic policies, transparency, and good governance in fostering sustainable economic growth. By analyzing Amin's economic missteps, policymakers can learn valuable lessons and strive to avoid similar pitfalls in their own countries.

In conclusion, Idi Amin's economic policies had a devastating impact on Uganda's economy. His mismanagement, corruption, and misguided policies resulted in a decline in productivity, inflation, and scarcity of essential goods. The legacy of Amin's economic misrule serves as a reminder of the importance of good governance and sound economic policies in fostering sustainable economic development.

Chapter 7: Idi Amin's Military Strategies and Conflicts during His Reign

Amin's Military Expansion and Modernization

The chapter "Amin's Military Expansion and Modernization" delves into one of the most crucial aspects of Idi Amin's rise to power and his subsequent reign as dictator of Uganda. This subchapter aims to provide politicians and diplomats with a comprehensive understanding of Amin's military strategies, conflicts, and their broader implications for African politics and post-colonial history.

Idi Amin's military career began early in his life, as he joined the King's African Rifles (KAR) in the late 1940s. His exceptional physical strength and leadership skills caught the attention of his superiors, propelling him through the ranks of the Ugandan military. This subchapter explores Amin's early experiences in the KAR, highlighting the formative years that shaped his military mindset and ambitions.

As Amin ascended to power, he prioritized military expansion and modernization. He significantly increased the military's budget, acquiring advanced weaponry and expanding the armed forces to solidify his grip on power. Amin's military strategies during his reign were characterized by a mix of calculated brutality and unpredictable decision-making. The subchapter examines key conflicts, such as the invasion of Tanzania, the persecution of political opponents, and the human rights abuses committed by his military forces.

Moreover, Amin's relationship with foreign powers and international politics had a profound impact on Uganda's trajectory. The subchapter delves into his volatile alliances with countries such as Libya, Saudi Arabia, and Israel, and how these relationships influenced both his domestic policies and his standing on the global stage.

Amin's cultural and religious impact on Uganda is another crucial aspect explored in this subchapter. His embrace of Islam and his efforts to align Uganda with the Arab world had far-reaching consequences for the country's social fabric and religious landscape. Additionally, his economic policies, which included nationalization and expulsion of Asian communities, had a detrimental effect on Uganda's economy, resulting in severe inflation and economic decline.

The subchapter also delves into Amin's military strategies and conflicts during his reign, including the Uganda-Tanzania War and his failed attempts to annex parts of Kenya. These military endeavors not only resulted in significant loss of life but also strained Uganda's diplomatic relations and isolated the country on the international stage.

Finally, the subchapter explores Amin's exile and life after being overthrown as dictator, his portrayal in literature, film, and popular culture, and his enduring legacy in African politics and post-colonial history. Through a thorough examination of these topics, politicians and diplomats will gain valuable insights into the complex and controversial figure that was Idi Amin, as well as the impact his military expansion and modernization had on Uganda and the wider region.

Amin's Involvement in Regional Conflicts

Idi Amin's reign as the dictator of Uganda was marked by his active involvement in regional conflicts, which had far-reaching consequences for the African continent. This subchapter aims to shed light on Amin's role in these conflicts and analyze their implications for both Uganda and its neighboring countries.

One of the most significant regional conflicts during Amin's rule was the Uganda-Tanzania War that took place from 1978 to 1979. Amin's aggressive foreign policy and territorial ambitions led him to invade Tanzania, which ultimately resulted in a swift and decisive defeat for the Ugandan military. This conflict not only exposed Amin's military weaknesses but also strained Uganda's relationship with its neighboring countries, leading to a complete breakdown of diplomatic ties.

Furthermore, Amin's involvement in the conflict in neighboring Sudan added fuel to the fire. He supported the southern Sudanese rebels, exacerbating the already complex internal dynamics of Sudan. Amin's intervention not only escalated tensions within Sudan but also strained Uganda's relationship with Sudan's government, which had severe implications for regional stability.

Amin's support for armed groups seeking to overthrow the governments of Kenya and Tanzania further intensified regional conflicts. His backing of the separatist group, the Mombasa Republican Council, in Kenya and the Zanzibar Liberation Front in Tanzania, destabilized these countries and threatened their territorial integrity.

In addition to his direct involvement in regional conflicts, Amin's regime became a safe haven for various militant groups. He provided shelter and support to organizations such as the Palestine Liberation Organization (PLO) and the Popular Front for the Liberation of Palestine (PFLP), which further strained Uganda's relations with Israel and Western powers.

The consequences of Amin's involvement in regional conflicts were profound. Uganda's economy suffered greatly due to the diversion of resources towards military endeavors, exacerbating the already dire economic situation. Moreover, the conflicts led to a massive influx of refugees into Uganda, placing immense strain on the country's limited resources.

Amin's involvement in regional conflicts also tarnished Uganda's reputation on the international stage. The brutalities committed by his regime, coupled with his disregard for human rights, drew widespread condemnation from the international community. This further isolated Uganda and had a lasting impact on its diplomatic relations.

In conclusion, Amin's involvement in regional conflicts had a significant impact on Uganda and its neighboring countries. The consequences of his military interventions were far-reaching, with severe implications for regional stability, Uganda's economy, and its international standing. Understanding Amin's role in these conflicts is crucial for politicians and diplomats to comprehend the complex dynamics of African politics during this period and to learn from the mistakes of the past.

Amin's Military Tactics and Legacy in the Armed Forces

Idi Amin's military tactics and legacy in the armed forces played a crucial role in shaping his rise to power and his brutal regime. In this subchapter, we will delve into the strategies Amin employed during his reign, their impact on Uganda, and his historical significance in African politics and post-colonial history.

Amin's military career began in the British colonial army, where he quickly rose through the ranks due to his natural leadership abilities and physical strength. His childhood and early life in Uganda provided him with a deep understanding of the local terrain and culture, which he cleverly utilized in his military strategies.

During his rise through the ranks of the Ugandan military, Amin employed a combination of charisma, fear, and manipulation to gain the loyalty of his subordinates. He strategically placed trusted allies in key positions, ensuring his control over the armed forces. Amin's military strategies were marked by aggression and unpredictability, which allowed him to maintain a strong grip on power and suppress any opposition.

However, Amin's military tactics also resulted in widespread human rights abuses and a reign of terror. His brutal regime was characterized by extrajudicial killings, torture, and mass displacement of certain ethnic groups. These actions not only devastated the lives of thousands of Ugandans but also tarnished Amin's reputation on the international stage.

Amin's relationship with foreign powers and international politics further shaped his military strategies. He played on Cold War rivalries and aligned himself with countries like Libya and the Soviet Union, receiving military aid in return. This support bolstered his military capabilities and allowed him to pursue aggressive policies, such as the invasion of Tanzania.

In addition to his military prowess, Amin's cultural and religious impact on Uganda cannot be overlooked. He promoted Islam and adopted a pan-Africanist stance, portraying himself as a champion of African unity. This resonated with certain segments of the population, further consolidating his power.

The economic policies implemented during Amin's reign had disastrous consequences for Uganda's economy. His nationalization and expulsion of Asian business owners led to a collapse of industries and a decline in foreign investment. The country was left in economic ruin, further exacerbating the suffering of the Ugandan people.

After being overthrown as dictator, Amin spent the rest of his life in exile, living between Saudi Arabia and Libya. Despite his brutal regime, Amin's portrayal in literature, film, and popular culture often romanticizes him or focuses on his eccentricities, overshadowing the immense suffering he inflicted.

Today, Amin's legacy remains a contentious issue. Some argue that his brutal reign and human rights abuses make him a symbol of tyranny. Others, however, believe that his rise to power and military strategies highlight the complexities of African politics and post-colonial history.

Understanding Amin's military tactics and legacy in the armed forces is crucial for politicians and diplomats to navigate the challenges of contemporary African politics and to prevent history from repeating itself.

Chapter 8: Idi Amin's Exile and Life after Being Overthrown as Dictator

Amin's Escape and Life in Exile

In the subchapter titled "Amin's Escape and Life in Exile," we delve into the dramatic turn of events that marked the downfall of Idi Amin's brutal regime and his subsequent life in exile. This period not only highlights the personal experiences of Amin but also sheds light on the complex web of international politics and the legacy he left behind in African politics.

After ruling Uganda with an iron fist for eight years, Amin's regime was marred by widespread human rights abuses and economic turmoil. Faced with mounting pressure from both domestic opposition and international condemnation, Amin's grip on power began to weaken.

In 1979, as rebel forces closed in on the capital city of Kampala, Amin's regime crumbled. Sensing imminent defeat, Amin made a daring escape, fleeing the country disguised as a pilot. This escape marked the end of his reign of terror but also the beginning of a new chapter in his life.

Once in exile, Amin sought refuge in various countries, including Libya, Saudi Arabia, and finally, in Equatorial Guinea. Despite his exile, Amin continued to be a controversial figure, with his actions and policies haunting him in the court of public opinion. His brutal regime and human rights abuses left a lasting scar on Uganda, and the international community closely monitored his movements.

During his time in exile, Amin's relationship with foreign powers and international politics remained a topic of interest. Despite being shunned by many nations, Amin continued to engage in political activities, seeking support and allies. His attempts to regain power were met with little success, as many countries were hesitant to associate themselves with his tainted legacy.

The impact of Amin's cultural and religious ideologies on Uganda cannot be ignored. Throughout his rule, Amin's policies favored his own ethnic group and fueled tribal tensions. His regime promoted a radical form of Islam, causing divisions and further destabilizing the country.

Furthermore, Amin's economic policies wreaked havoc on Uganda's economy. His reckless nationalization of industries and expulsion of Asian Ugandans resulted in economic collapse. The effects of these policies were felt long after his reign, with Uganda struggling to recover from the damage caused.

In conclusion, Amin's escape and subsequent life in exile were marked by political isolation and a tarnished reputation. His brutal regime, human rights abuses, and economic mismanagement left an indelible mark on Uganda. Despite his attempts to regain power and rewrite his legacy, Amin's portrayal in literature, film, and popular culture has cemented his image as one of the most despised dictators in history. His legacy and historical significance lie in serving as a cautionary tale of the dangers of unchecked power and the need for strong institutions in African politics and post-colonial history.

Amin's Attempts at Regaining Power

In the subchapter "Amin's Attempts at Regaining Power," we delve into the intriguing and tumultuous post-dictatorship period of Idi Amin's life. This phase was marked by Amin's relentless efforts to regain power and the subsequent political dynamics that unfolded in Uganda and on the international stage. This chapter explores the intricate web of events, strategies, and alliances that characterized Amin's pursuit of authority, shedding light on the consequences for Uganda and the wider African political landscape.

Following his ousting from power in 1979, Amin's thirst for control remained unquenched. Despite being exiled in Saudi Arabia, he plotted his return to Uganda, seeking support from various quarters. Amin capitalized on his charisma and manipulation skills to rally loyalists within the Ugandan military and exploit existing divisions within the nation. These attempts at regaining power were met with fierce resistance from Ugandan politicians and diplomats, who were committed to preventing a return to the brutal regime that had plagued their country.

Amin's international relationships played a crucial role in his endeavors. He skillfully navigated the complex arena of international politics, exploiting Cold War rivalries and capitalizing on his connections with certain foreign powers. He courted support from Libya's Muammar Gaddafi and other sympathetic nations, using their backing to strengthen his position within Uganda and further his ambitions. However, the international community, including politicians and diplomats from various countries, vehemently opposed his return to power, fearing a resurgence of Amin's human rights abuses and destabilizing influence.

Simultaneously, Amin's cultural and religious impact on Uganda continued to reverberate. His regime had exacerbated ethnic tensions and religious divisions, leaving a lasting impact on the nation's social fabric. Politicians and diplomats grappled with the challenge of reconciling these deep-rooted divisions while ensuring a peaceful transition and preventing a reemergence of Amin's divisive policies.

Moreover, Amin's economic policies and military strategies during his reign had left Uganda in dire straits. His attempts at regaining power were also motivated by the desire to regain control over Uganda's economy and its natural resources. However, his brutal regime had devastated the economy, leading to widespread poverty and instability. Politicians and diplomats were confronted with the task of rebuilding the nation's economy and ensuring sustainable development while simultaneously preventing Amin's return to power.

Ultimately, Amin's attempts at regaining power were thwarted. His exile in Saudi Arabia became a permanent arrangement, and he spent the rest of his life there. Despite his fall from power, Amin's legacy continued to shape Uganda and the African political landscape. His brutal regime and human rights abuses left an indelible mark on the collective memory of Ugandans and served as a stark reminder of the dangers posed by dictatorial regimes. Politicians and diplomats grappled with the challenge of reconciling this dark chapter in Uganda's history while striving for a brighter future.

In conclusion, "Amin's Attempts at Regaining Power" sheds light on the tumultuous post-dictatorship period in Idi Amin's life. This subchapter explores the intricacies of Amin's pursuit of authority, his relationships with foreign powers, the impact of his regime on Uganda, and the lasting consequences for African politics. It serves as a cautionary tale for politicians and diplomats, reminding them of the importance of upholding human rights, fostering political stability, and preventing the resurgence of oppressive regimes.

Amin's Death and Funeral

The death and funeral of Idi Amin marked the end of an era characterized by brutal dictatorship, human rights abuses, and economic decline. Amin's demise not only brought relief to the people of Uganda but also had significant implications for international politics and the post-colonial history of Africa.

Amin's death on August 16, 2003, marked the end of his reign of terror that lasted from 1971 to 1979. Politicians and diplomats, who had been closely monitoring his regime, were both intrigued and relieved by the news. Amin's childhood and early life in Uganda, which shaped his character and leadership style, were now scrutinized to understand the roots of his tyrannical rule.

As a military officer, Amin rose through the ranks swiftly, taking advantage of political instability and tribal tensions in Uganda. His military strategies and conflicts during his reign were marked by brutal and ruthless tactics, resulting in the deaths of thousands of innocent civilians. International powers and foreign governments, including the United States and the United Kingdom, had varying relationships with Amin, oscillating between support and condemnation.

Amin's brutal regime and human rights abuses left a lasting impact on Uganda. His reign was characterized by arbitrary arrests, torture, and extrajudicial killings. The funeral of such a despised leader was therefore a complex event, with politicians and diplomats navigating the delicate balance between acknowledging the passing of a former head of state and respecting the victims of Amin's atrocities.

While Amin's cultural and religious impact on Uganda was significant, with his promotion of Islam and persecution of certain ethnic groups, it was his economic policies that plunged the country into a deep recession. His nationalization and mismanagement of industries led to hyperinflation, unemployment, and widespread poverty.

Following his overthrow in 1979, Amin lived in exile, primarily in Saudi Arabia, until his death. His portrayal in literature, film, and popular culture further solidified his reputation as one of history's most brutal dictators. From novels to movies, Amin became a symbol of tyranny and human rights abuses.

Idi Amin's legacy and historical significance in African politics and post-colonial history cannot be underestimated. His regime serves as a stark reminder of the dangers of unchecked power and the importance of upholding human rights. Amin's death and funeral marked the end of an era of fear and oppression, offering an opportunity for Uganda to heal and rebuild. For politicians and diplomats, it was a moment of reflection and a reminder of the importance of international intervention in preventing the rise of future dictators.

Chapter 9: Idi Amin's Portrayal in Literature, Film, and Popular Culture

Amin's Representation in Fictional Works

Idi Amin's journey through the ranks of the Ugandan military and his subsequent rise to power as a dictator have left an indelible mark on Uganda and the rest of the world. His brutal regime, human rights abuses, and controversial political decisions have been subjects of intense scrutiny and analysis. However, alongside the factual accounts of Amin's reign, his life and legacy have also been explored in the realm of fiction, offering a unique perspective on his character and impact.

In various literary works, films, and popular culture, Amin's portrayal ranges from sympathetic to scathing, from nuanced to caricature-like. These fictional representations provide a space for artists and writers to delve into the complexities of his personality, the motivations behind his actions, and the broader implications of his rule.

Through the lens of fiction, politicians and diplomats can gain a deeper understanding of the psychological factors that contributed to Amin's rise to power and the subsequent impact on Uganda's political landscape. By exploring the fictionalized accounts, they can better comprehend the social, cultural, and economic factors that shaped Amin's regime and its consequences.

Moreover, Amin's representation in fictional works often sheds light on his relationships with foreign powers and their involvement in Ugandan politics during his reign. By examining these portrayals, politicians and diplomats can gain insight into the intricate dynamics of international politics and how they influenced Amin's decision-making processes.

Furthermore, the impact of Amin's cultural and religious identity on Uganda is also explored in fictional works. Authors and filmmakers delve into the role of Amin's ethnicity and religious background in shaping his policies, as well as the broader implications for Ugandan society.

Additionally, fictional accounts delve into Amin's economic policies and their effects on Uganda's economy, offering an opportunity for politicians and diplomats to examine the long-term consequences of his decisions. By understanding the fictionalized portrayals, they can analyze the economic challenges faced by the country during Amin's reign and draw lessons for contemporary economic policies.

Furthermore, Amin's military strategies and conflicts during his reign are often depicted in fictional works, allowing politicians and diplomats to analyze the tactics employed and the consequences for Uganda's security and stability.

Lastly, the portrayal of Amin in literature, film, and popular culture helps to understand the legacy and historical significance of his rule in African politics and post-colonial history. By examining these representations, politicians and diplomats can gain insights into how Amin's reign continues to shape the collective memory and perception of Uganda's past.

In conclusion, the fictional representation of Idi Amin offers a valuable perspective for politicians and diplomats seeking to comprehend the complexities of his life, regime, and legacy. By exploring these works, they can gain a deeper understanding of the psychological, cultural, and political factors that contributed to Amin's rise and reign, as well as the broader implications for Uganda and African politics.

Amin's Depiction in Documentary Films

Amin's reign as dictator of Uganda from 1971 to 1979 was marked by brutality, human rights abuses, and a disregard for international norms.

His volatile personality, erratic behavior, and ruthless tactics made him a controversial figure on the global stage. Amin's story has been extensively covered in various forms of media, including documentary films that aim to shed light on his complex character and the impact of his regime.

Documentary films have been a powerful tool to educate and inform the public, including politicians and diplomats, about the atrocities committed by Amin and his regime. These films provide an in-depth analysis of Amin's childhood and early life in Uganda, tracing his journey through the ranks of the Ugandan military. They explore the factors that contributed to his rise to power, such as his charisma, military prowess, and manipulation of political alliances.

Through interviews with survivors, witnesses, and experts, these films highlight the brutal nature of Amin's regime and the gross human rights abuses that were perpetrated under his rule. They delve into the mechanisms of oppression, including torture, extrajudicial killings, and the suppression of dissent. By examining the testimonies of those who suffered at the hands of Amin and his henchmen, these documentaries aim to ensure that such atrocities are not forgotten or repeated.

Amin's relationship with foreign powers and international politics is another crucial aspect explored in these films. They delve into his alliances with various countries, including Libya and the Soviet Union, and the impacts of these relationships on Uganda's political landscape. These documentaries examine the international community's response to Amin's regime and the challenges faced by diplomats and politicians as they grappled with how to deal with his oppressive rule.

Moreover, these films shed light on Amin's cultural and religious impact on Uganda. They explore the manipulation of tribal and religious tensions to advance his political agenda and maintain control over the diverse population. Additionally, they analyze Amin's economic policies and their detrimental effects on Uganda's economy, which ultimately led to its decline and instability.

Furthermore, documentary films provide insights into Amin's military strategies and conflicts during his reign. They examine his involvement in regional conflicts, such as the war with Tanzania and the attempted invasion of Kenya, and the consequences of these military adventures on Uganda and its neighboring countries.

Beyond Amin's time in power, these films also explore his exile and life after being overthrown as dictator. They reveal his attempts to regain influence, his life in Saudi Arabia, and the controversies surrounding his death and burial.

The portrayal of Amin in literature, film, and popular culture is a fascinating aspect that these documentaries delve into. They analyze the impact of films such as "The Last King of Scotland" and "General Idi Amin Dada: A Self Portrait" on shaping public perception and understanding of Amin's character.

Finally, these films examine Amin's legacy and historical significance in African politics and post-colonial history. They assess the long-lasting impacts of his regime on Uganda, including the deep scars left on the nation's psyche and the challenges faced in the process of reconciliation and justice.

In conclusion, documentary films offer a comprehensive and detailed exploration of Amin's life, reign, and legacy. By addressing the niches of Idi Amin's childhood and early life, rise through the ranks of the military, brutal regime and human rights abuses, relationship with foreign powers, cultural and religious impact, economic policies, military strategies, exile and life after being overthrown, portrayal in literature and film, as well as his historical significance, these documentaries provide politicians, diplomats, and the wider audience with a deeper understanding of one of Africa's most notorious dictators.

Amin's Pop Culture References and Influence

Idi Amin Dada, the notorious dictator of Uganda, not only left a trail of human rights abuses and economic devastation, but also made a lasting impact on popular culture both within Uganda and around the world. From literature and film to music and fashion, Amin's influence can be seen in various facets of the global entertainment industry.

In literature, Amin's brutal regime and the atrocities committed during his rule have been depicted in numerous works. Writers such as V.S. Naipaul, Giles Foden, and Ryszard Kapuscinski have explored the dark underbelly of Amin's dictatorship, shedding light on the human suffering and political turmoil that characterized his reign. These literary accounts have not only served as a historical record but have also contributed to shaping the global perception of Amin and his regime.

Film has also played a significant role in perpetuating Amin's legacy. The 2006 film "The Last King of Scotland," based on Giles Foden's novel, showcased Forest Whitaker's mesmerizing portrayal of Amin, earning him an Academy Award for Best Actor. This film brought Amin's story to a wider audience, sparking renewed interest in his dictatorship and the impact it had on Uganda and its people.

In popular music, Amin's influence can be seen through the emergence of songs and albums that address his regime and its consequences. Artists such as Bobi Wine, a Ugandan musician turned politician, have used their music as a powerful tool to critique the injustices of Amin's era and advocate for social change. These artists have not only kept the memory of Amin alive but have also contributed to the ongoing struggle for justice and human rights in Uganda.

Even in fashion, Amin's impact can be felt. His flamboyant military uniforms and eccentric style have inspired designers and fashion enthusiasts around the world. From runway shows to magazine spreads, elements of Amin's fashion choices have been incorporated into modern trends, adding a touch of his unique aesthetic to the world of haute couture.

In conclusion, Idi Amin's influence extends far beyond the political sphere. His brutal regime and the human rights abuses committed during his rule have made a lasting impact on literature, film, music, fashion, and popular culture in general. Understanding Amin's cultural and historical significance is crucial not only for politicians and diplomats but also for anyone interested in African politics and post-colonial history. By examining Amin's pop culture references and influence, we gain a deeper understanding of the complex legacy left by one of Africa's most notorious dictators.

Chapter 10: Idi Amin's Legacy and Historical Significance in African Politics and Post-Colonial History

Amin's Impact on Ugandan Politics and Society

Idi Amin's journey through the ranks of the Ugandan military left an indelible mark on the country's politics and society. This subchapter delves into the various aspects of Amin's impact, exploring the significant events and policies that shaped Uganda during his brutal regime.

Starting with Amin's childhood and early life in Uganda, it becomes evident that his upbringing played a crucial role in shaping his character and political ideology. Born to a rural family, Amin's humble origins allowed him to connect with the common people, which later influenced his populist approach to governance.

Amin's rise through the ranks of the Ugandan military was marked by ambition and ruthlessness. His ability to manipulate and eliminate potential rivals allowed him to seize power in a military coup, overthrowing President Obote. This chapter examines the strategies employed by Amin to consolidate his power and maintain control over the military and the nation.

Central to Amin's reign were his brutal regime and human rights abuses. The subchapter exposes the horrifying details of his reign, including mass killings, torture, and forced disappearances. The impact of these atrocities on Ugandan society was profound, as fear and repression became pervasive.

Amin's relationship with foreign powers and international politics also had far-reaching consequences. His alliances with certain countries, such as Libya and Saudi Arabia, provided him with economic support and diplomatic cover, while his anti-Western rhetoric and expulsion of Asians strained relations with other nations. This subchapter explores the complexities of Amin's foreign policy and its implications for Uganda.

Additionally, Amin's cultural and religious impact on Uganda is examined. His promotion of Islam as the state religion and the persecution of certain ethnic groups fostered division and sectarianism. The subchapter also explores the influence of Amin's eccentric personality on Ugandan culture, as he sought to create a larger-than-life image through propaganda and media manipulation.

Furthermore, Amin's economic policies and their effects on Uganda's economy are analyzed. His nationalization of key industries and expulsion of foreign investors resulted in economic decline and widespread poverty. The chapter delves into the long-term consequences of Amin's economic mismanagement and the challenges faced during the post-Amin era.

Militarily, Amin's reign was marked by conflicts and strategic decisions. This subchapter examines his military strategies, including the invasion of Tanzania and the failed attempt to annex parts of Kenya. It also explores the impact of these conflicts on Uganda's regional standing and international reputation.

The subchapter concludes with an exploration of Amin's exile and life after being overthrown as dictator. Despite his eventual fall from power, Amin continued to make headlines with his controversial statements and attempts to regain influence. His life in exile shed light on his character and the lasting legacy he left behind.

Finally, Amin's portrayal in literature, film, and popular culture is discussed. His larger-than-life personality and brutal rule have been subjects of numerous books, movies, and artistic creations. This subchapter examines the various narratives surrounding Amin and their impact on public perception.

In conclusion, Idi Amin's impact on Ugandan politics and society was profound and far-reaching. This subchapter delves into the different facets of his rule, offering a comprehensive understanding of his childhood, rise to power, brutal regime, international relations, cultural impact, economic policies, military strategies, exile, portrayal in popular culture, and lasting legacy. By examining these aspects, politicians and diplomats can gain valuable insights into the complexities of African politics and post-colonial history.

Amin's Influence on African Dictators and Power Structures

Idi Amin, the notorious dictator who ruled Uganda from 1971 to 1979, left an indelible mark on not only the nation but also on the wider African continent. This subchapter explores Amin's influence on African dictators and power structures, shedding light on the lasting impact his regime had on politics, human rights, international relations, culture, and economics.

Amin's rise to power was a result of his cunning and manipulation within the Ugandan military. Born in rural Uganda, Amin's childhood and early life shaped his character and ambition. His ability to exploit ethnic divisions and promote himself as a defender of the marginalized enabled him to ascend through the ranks of the military and eventually seize control.

Once in power, Amin unleashed a reign of terror marked by brutal human rights abuses. His regime was characterized by rampant violence, torture, and extrajudicial killings. These atrocities had a profound impact on the political landscape in Africa, inspiring other dictators to emulate Amin's methods of consolidating power through fear and violence.

Amin's relationship with foreign powers and international politics further solidified his influence. He skillfully played off Cold War rivalries, shifting alliances to his advantage. Amin's support from certain Western countries and his alignment with Arab nations influenced the dynamics of power in the region and highlighted the complexities of international relations during the era.

Moreover, Amin's cultural and religious impact on Uganda cannot be understated. His policies of favoring certain ethnic groups and his conversion to Islam significantly altered the social fabric of the country. This had far-reaching consequences on the relationship between different ethnic and religious communities, resulting in long-standing tensions that continue to shape Ugandan society today.

Economically, Amin's policies were disastrous for Uganda. His ill-conceived plans and mismanagement led to economic decline, hyperinflation, and widespread poverty. The effects of Amin's economic policies on Uganda's economy reverberated long after his ousting, leaving a legacy of economic challenges that the country continues to grapple with.

Militarily, Amin's strategies and conflicts during his reign showcased his penchant for aggression and expansionism. His invasion of neighboring Tanzania in 1978, known as the Uganda-Tanzania War, led to his eventual downfall and exile. Amin's military escapades demonstrated the dangers of unchecked power and the impact of regional conflicts on African politics.

Following his overthrow, Amin lived in exile, primarily in Saudi Arabia, until his death in 2003. His post-dictatorship life offers insights into the complexities of dealing with former dictators and their legacies. Furthermore, Amin's portrayal in literature, film, and popular culture has perpetuated his image as a ruthless dictator, contributing to the understanding of his reign and its consequences.

In conclusion, Idi Amin's influence on African dictators and power structures extended far beyond his time in office. His brutal regime, manipulation of international politics, and impact on Ugandan society and economy continue to shape African politics and post-colonial history. Understanding Amin's legacy is essential for politicians and diplomats in navigating the challenges posed by authoritarian regimes and creating a more just and stable future in Africa.

Amin's Historical Evaluation and Lessons Learned

Idi Amin Dada, the notorious dictator who ruled Uganda from 1971 to 1979, left an indelible mark on the history of African politics and post-colonial history. His rise to power, brutal regime, and human rights abuses have had far-reaching consequences, making it imperative for politicians and diplomats to study and understand his historical evaluation. By examining Amin's childhood, early life, rise through the ranks of the Ugandan military, and his impact on various aspects of Ugandan society, valuable lessons can be learned.

Idi Amin's childhood and early life in Uganda laid the foundation for his later actions. Born in Koboko, a remote village in northwestern Uganda, Amin experienced poverty and marginalization. His upbringing, although challenging, provided insights into the socio-economic issues that plagued Uganda during the post-colonial era. Understanding these early struggles helps politicians and diplomats comprehend the factors that contributed to Amin's rise to power.

Amin's ascent through the ranks of the Ugandan military was marked by cunning political maneuvers and ruthlessness. By studying his military strategies and conflicts during his reign, valuable lessons can be learned about the potential dangers of unchecked power. Amin's brutal regime and human rights abuses, including the ethnic cleansing of various communities, emphasize the importance of safeguarding human rights and the need for international intervention in such cases.

The relationship between Amin and foreign powers, as well as his impact on international politics, is another crucial aspect to evaluate. Amin's alignment with the Arab world and his anti-Israel stance strained Uganda's relationships with Western countries. This examination helps politicians and diplomats understand the complexities of balancing international alliances and the significance of diplomatic efforts in preventing human rights abuses.

Amin's cultural and religious impact on Uganda cannot be overlooked. His policies favored certain ethnic groups while marginalizing others, leading to deep-seated divisions within Ugandan society. This evaluation highlights the importance of promoting inclusivity and tolerance in diverse societies, as well as the negative consequences of using religion and ethnicity for political gain.

Furthermore, examining Amin's economic policies and their effects on Uganda's economy provides valuable insights into the dangers of reckless decision-making. Amin's nationalization and mismanagement of industries resulted in economic decline and widespread poverty. This evaluation underscores the need for sound economic policies and competent governance to ensure the well-being of a nation.

Finally, Amin's exile and life after being overthrown as a dictator shed light on the complexities of post-dictatorship transitions. His portrayal in literature, film, and popular culture highlights the lasting impact of his regime on Uganda's collective memory. Understanding these portrayals can help politicians and diplomats navigate the challenges of transitional justice and reconciliation processes.

In conclusion, Amin's historical evaluation and the lessons learned from his dictatorial regime are of utmost importance to politicians and diplomats. By delving into his childhood, rise to power, brutal regime, and impact on various aspects of Ugandan society, valuable insights can be gained. These lessons serve as a reminder of the importance of safeguarding human rights, promoting inclusivity, and fostering competent governance in order to prevent the rise of dictators and ensure a prosperous future for nations.